SPEECH

OF

BENJAMIN BARSTOW,

OF SALEM,

ON THE

ABOLITION PROPENSITIES

OF

CALEB CUSHING.

Delivered at the Massachusetts National Democratic Convention, held at Boston, Sept. 22, 1853.

TO

FRANKLIN PIERCE:

—— —— Our chief of men, who, through a cloud
Not of war only, but detractions rude,
Guided by faith and matchless fortitude,
To peace and truth thy glorious way hast ploughed.
* * * * * *
—— —— —— —— —— Yet much remains
To conquer still; Peace hath her victories,
No less renowned than War; new foes arise,
Threatening to bind our souls in secular chains.
Help us to save free conscience from the paw
Of hireling wolves whose gospel is their maw.

[MILTON—SONNET TO CROMWELL.

BOSTON:
PUBLISHED AT THE OFFICE OF THE NATIONAL DEMOCRAT,
No. 15 Brattle Street.
1853.

SPEECH.

The National Democratic State Convention for Massachusetts met at Boston, at the Tremont Temple, September 22d, 1853.

After the organization and the choice of Committees, Mr. BENJAMIN BARSTOW of Salem rose to make a personal explanation, requesting the indulgence of the Convention therefor.

The President decided that leave must be requested of the Convention, and, on motion, Mr. Barstow was allowed to proceed. He spoke as follows:

Mr. President and Gentlemen:—I rise to a personal question, to make an explanation, and, as it may occupy some time, I ask your indulgence. I have been informed that I have been denounced to different members of the State Committee, and the National Democratic party of Massachusetts, for opinions which I saw fit to express during the early part of March last, in reference to the Hon. Caleb Cushing, while I was on a visit to Washington; and it has been stated that the State Committee and the whole party should be held responsible for what I said. Under these circumstances, feeling that I may have involved you and those you represent, I feel bound to state to you what I did say, and to give you my reasons for doing so

Upon the announcement that the Hon. Caleb Cushing was to be a member of the Cabinet, feeling indignant that the National Democracy of New England should be so misrepresented as it would be by one whose career for the greater part of his life has been in the Whig party, and whom I believe at the present time to be as much a Whig as ever, I accused him openly of being such, and also what is equally well known in Massachusetts, — of being a Coalitionist. For this, it seems, I incurred the wrath of that gentleman, and members of the State Committee were told by him that unless they stopped "that beardless boy," the whole party should be held responsible. If Gen. Cushing thinks a "beardless man" a finer looking object than a "beardless boy," he is welcome to his taste; but as to the charge of youth, I will say, that it has been my good fortune to have been a member of the Democratic party for twenty-four years longer than Caleb Cushing, even taking his own dates, and I have only to refer him to his own defence against the same charge, in a statement over his name, accompanying a certain *notorious affidavit* in 1826, in which he says:

"I am also accused of youth and ambition. As for the heinous fault of not being an old man, I may say with Chatham, in *his* youth, that I hope time will mend it; and that the charge comes with ill grace from some to whom age has arrived without wisdom. But in seriousness, it is needless to be wiser than the constitution."

Before proceeding with the charges I made against General Cushing, I wish to call your attention to the gross injustice of attempting to throw upon my shoulders, and to attribute to any remarks of mine, a line of policy which extends throughout the whole North, and was determined upon a long time previously. I wish also to state, to avoid any false imputations, that I have never been an applicant for any office, State or national, directly or indirectly, nor has my name ever been used as such, to my knowledge; and in reference to the coalition, I will say, that in 1849, when it was first formed, believing it to extend to State purposes alone, I warmly adopted it; but immediately upon discovering its connexion with the slavery question, I as warmly opposed it, and have done so ever since.

And now, gentlemen, I charge Caleb Cushing with deceiving the President, with being a Whig, a Coalitionist, and abolition agitator.

And first, as to deceiving the President. Let us see what Franklin Pierce stood pledged to do upon commencing his administrative career. If he has pledged himself to one thing, and has done another, either he has broken his promises or he has been deceived in his agents.

In the summer or fall of 1850, the Democratic party of New Hampshire, under the immediate lead of Franklin Pierce, assembled in State Convention, and rejecting John Atwood, the nominee of the regular annual convention, nominated another gentleman in his place. Why? Because John Atwood and his friends had formed a coalition with the Free Soilers of New Hampshire, for the purpose of electing that gentleman Governor of the State, and of defeating the operation of the compromise measures, and the Democratic party. By so doing, General Pierce obtained the confidence of the Union men of the country, and succeeded eventually in becoming President By this he pledged himself against coalitions with Free Soilers and in favor of the National Democracy.

In the spring of 1851, the coalition in Massachusetts, which had been formed the previous fall, was perfected by an agreement made on the 6th day of January between the Free Soil and Democratic representatives in the Legislature, to the effect that Chas Sumner should receive the votes of the Democratic party for United States Senator. The Democracy of the city of Salem held a meeting on the 7th day of that month—the ensuing evening—and passed a series of resolutions denouncing the bargain as a fraud upon the Democracy, one of which resolutions was as follows:

Resolved, That all those who assent to any such bargain or consent to pay any such price, must bear in mind that any Freesoil Senator, if elected, would be necessarily an opponent of the next administration, should that administration be—as it probably will be—Democratic, and that all those who class themselves as the friends of such a Senator, and who are instrumental in his election, must necessarily also be opponents of the next Democratic administration, and of the distinguished men of whom it is composed, and by whom it will be supported, and must be prepared to take all the necessary consequences of that position.

These resolutions were published in the *Boston Post* of the 9th of January, and the mail from Concord next ensuing brought a letter from Gen. Pierce written with his characteristic impulsiveness, warmly approving the resolutions, and the stand taken by the Salem Democracy, saying—"He was so pleased he could not help sitting down to let us know," and complimenting us strongly on our Democracy and patriotism.

Here was a virtual adhesion to the policy laid down in the resolutions, and it sustained us in our unwavering opposition to the Coalition.

The Baltimore Convention met in June, 1852, and adopted a platform warmly sustaining the Compromise measures, and deciding that no one who opposed those measures belonged to the Democratic party. As if to leave no room for doubt as to their meaning, they proceeded to reject the Hon. Robert Rantoul, Jr., a leading Coalitionist and Free Soil Democrat, solely upon the ground of his opinions on the compromise measures, and his part in the Massachusetts Coalition, and this too by the decisive vote of 194 to 83, thus leaving no room to doubt that the compromise measures formed an essential part of the Democratic creed.

Gen. Pierce, in accepting the nomination then tendered to him, says, in his letter of June 17th, 1852—"May I not regard it as a fact pointing to the overthrow of sectional jealousies," and proceeds to say—"I accept the nomination upon the platform adopted by the convention, not because this is expected of me as a candidate, but, because the principles it embraces command the approbation of my judgment; and with them, I believe I can safely say, there has been no word nor act of my life in conflict."

Thus again, in this last sentence, he pledges himself that the rejection of all coalitions with Free Soilers, and the proscription of such men as John Atwood, form part of the platform laid down at Baltimore, and will form part of his course if elected. Thus repeatedly he pledges himself to sustain pure national Democracy, untinctured by Free Soilism.

Now what has been the course of the Administration? Look at the appointments which have been made in this State. Multitudes of cases, known to all of you, might be brought up, to show the Free Soil inclinations of the appointing power, whoever that may be. I shall confine myself to what has been passing under my own eyes, and in my own county of Essex—the county of Caleb Cushing also.

On the 26th of May, Lewis Josselyn of Lynn was appointed the Surveyor of the port of Salem and Beverly. This Josselyn is too well known to require a long description. He has always been conspicuous for his Free Soil inclinations. He was an early and an able advocate for the coalition, and upon its success received the office of Clerk of the House of Representatives for himself, and Assistant Clerk for his son, which netted not far from $2000 a year; he has edited for some years the *Lynn Bay State*, a paper of the strongest Free Soil tendency, and as such, has commented freely upon the politics of this and the neighboring States. I shall select, as pertinent to the occasion, his paper of March 20, 1851, in which he comments upon the result of the election in New Hampshire, after the rejection of John Atwood. Now as this was Gen. Pierce's act, and as the President says in his letter accepting his nomination, that it was identical in principle with the Baltimore Platform, it will show the beautiful harmony between the President and his appointees:

"It is not a pleasant task for us, under any circumstances, to record the defeat of the Democracy in any State in the Union. But there are circumstances connected with the late election in the Granite State, and the defeat of the 'Old Hunker' Democrats, which go very far to make us reconciled with the result, and even to believe that 'it is all for the best,' and that 'great good will grow out of it.'"

It quotes from the *Manchester Democrat*, speaking of Franklin Pierce and others:

"When some ten weeks ago, certain *false-hearted* and *self-elected* Democratic leaders proclaimed that every man should be thrown overboard who would not vow to support the fugitive slave law, they were distinctly told that this step would bring defeat upon the party, and give at least two Congressional districts to the Whigs. But no—the commands of Daniel Webster and FRANKLIN PIERCE *must* be obeyed—the common people are insultingly told that they are incapable of judging of the merits of this law—the *bargain* at Franklin must be carried out, and the slaveholders must be propitiated."

Again the *Bay State* says:

"No set of leaders by offers of reward or threats of vengeance, can induce the mass of the Democratic party to abandon their cherished hopes of the advancement of Humanity, and their firm reliance on the eternal principles of Justice and Liberty, which are the foundation of true Democracy [of course the surveyorship will not induce Mr. Josselyn.] And we admire the spirit with which thousands of good and true Democrats in the Granite State have come forward in this election and have said to those who would reduce them to a political bondage as degrading as African slavery, 'Thus far shalt thou go and no further.'"

Again he says:

"Do the Democratic leaders in New Hampshire, or any other State, mean to make the 'compromise measures' and the *Fugitive Slave law* a test in the next Presidential election? Is every Democrat to be thrown over who is opposed to that 'bill of abominations?' It will be difficult to find a place large enough to put them in—and there would not be an omnibus full left of the party."

An announcement appeared in the Bay State that the editor was about to publish a daily paper in Salem, and shortly after, on the 26th of May, he received an appointment as Surveyor.

Another appointment is that of G. J. L Colby, editor of the *Newburyport Union*, who was appointed Storekeeper and Inspector at Salem, an office worth, by the Blue Book, near $1500 a year. This Colby was, as he says, a member of the Liberty party in 1842-3, and implies that he is of the same sentiments still, although he has no confidence in the men of that organization. He has also been accused of delivering Anti-Slavery lectures in various places, which he admits in his paper of June 16, 1853, and expresses strong approbation of the principles of the old Liberty party, and his sympathies have always been like Josselyn's. The *Union* newspaper, under his charge, has always been a strong advocate for the coalition, and being well known at Washington, he received his appointment. But I cannot resist the temptation to allude to one more appointment—that of George B. Loring, as Postmaster of Salem. This gentleman was a Candidate for Collector of that port, and his appointment was opposed by 99 out of a hundred of the party. A remonstrance was signed by 350 of the Coalition and National Democrats of Salem and Beverly, against his appointment, as being odious to the party and citizens generally, and the obliquity of his political course fully exposed. This was sent to Washington, but he was appointed Postmaster notwithstanding. This gentleman was a warm supporter of Robert Rantoul, Jr., till his death—a Vice President of the Lynn meeting, at which Mr. R. joined the Abolitionists—a warm Coalitionist and an eager office-seeker. At the Convention which chose a delegate, who unseated Mr. Rantoul at Baltimore, Mr. Loring made an idle and weak attempt to break up the Convention, of which he was not a member, but an intruder. Mr. Loring held two offices from the Coalition, as appears from the following letter from the Secretary of State, and became a furious National Democrat just a fortnight before the Presidential election:

SECRETARY'S OFFICE, Boston, January 22d, 1853.

Sir:—In answer to yours of the 21st inst., I am able to state that George B. Loring of Salem, was appointed a Commissioner July 3d, 1852, under a resolve of that year, ch. 98 providing "for the appointment of Commissioners to examine Cape Cod Harbor."

George B. Loring, of Chelsea, was appointed a Trustee of the School for training and teaching Idiots, June 16, 1851, and re-appointed May 14th, 1852.

Very respectfully, your ob't serv't,
E. M. WRIGHT,
Secretary of the Commonwealth.

BENJAMIN BARSTOW, Esq. Salem.

The *Commonwealth* newspaper, in Boston, in October 1852, says:

"We have in our possession an anti-slavery pamphlet written by Dr. Loring of Salem, not many years since, in opposition to some pro slavery articles in the *Boston Post*. Dr. Loring was then a respectable abolitionist. We do not clearly understand what has converted him into a Hunker Democrat. Some folks in Salem think they do."

This charge of authorship, though frequently reiterated in public prints and elsewhere, has never been denied by that gentleman. It has been my good fortune to procure a copy of this pamphlet, which fully justifies the remarks of the Commonwealth, but which I will spare you, having more important matter to lay before you.

The appointments of Messrs. Josselyn and Loring will come before the Senate in December.

The Hon. Caleb Cushing was selected to represent New England in the Cabinet. As a general thing, the appointments in each section of the country would necessarily be approved by the representative in the Cabinet, or he would resign. But we have particular proof of the interest felt in some of these appointments by the gentleman referred to.

The records of the City Clerk at Lynn show that the *Bay State* newspaper (Mr. Josselyn's) is under a mortgage to Hon. John B. Alley, the Free Soil candidate for Congress in 1852, for one thousand dollars, as appears by the following:

Know all men by these presents, that I, Lewis Josselyn, of Lynn, in the county of Essex, State of Massachusetts, in consideration of the sum of one thousand dollars, to me paid by John B. Alley, of said Lynn, the receipt whereof is hereby acknowledged, have granted, bargained and sold, and by these presents do grant, bargain, and sell unto the said Alley, the whole and entire printing establishment known as the *Bay State* office, situated in Union street, in said Lynn, being the same establishment which I purchased of John B. Tolman, October first, A. D. 1849, and of which a schedule appears in a mortgage made to the said Tolman, October 1st, 1849, and recorded in Lynn Town Records, Book 5, pages 72 to 77, which schedule is to be referred to as a part of this mortgage. To have and to hold the afore described goods and chattels, to the said Alley, to his executors, administrators, and assigns, forever. And I the said Josselyn, do avouch myself to be the lawful owner of said goods and chattels, and have good right to sell and dispose of the same in manner aforesaid.

Provided nevertheless, that if the said Lewis Josselyn, his executors, or administrators or assigns, shall pay unto the said Alley, his executors or administrators, the said sum of one thousand dollars, as follows, to wit —five hundred dollars in six months and five hundred in twelve months from the date hereof, then this mortgage, as also two promissory notes bearing even date herewith, signed by the said Josselyn, whereby he promises, &c., shall be void.

In witness whereof, I, the said Lewis Josselyn, have subscribed the same, this second day of October, in the year of our Lord one thousand eight hundred and fifty-one.

LEWIS JOSSELYN.

Executed and delivered in presence of J. R. NEWHALL.

Recorded October 7th, 1853, 30 minutes past 5, P. M.

Another mortgage from Lewis Josselyn to John B. Alley, dated June 14th, 1853, of—

The power printing press on which the *Bay State* newspaper is printed, together with all the types and other printing materials which have been added to the *Bay State* printing office in said Lynn, since the second day of October, A. D. 1851.

Provided nevertheless, that this conveyance shall be void and of no effect if the said Josselyn, his executors or administrators, shall pay unto the said Alley, his executors, and administrators or assigns, the sum of one thousand dollars and interest at the time following, to wit: on demand, and for which sum and interest, I, the said Josselyn, have given two promissory notes, bearing date Oct. 2d, 1851, signed by myself, and made payable to the said Alley or his order; one of said notes being made payable six months from its date, and the other in twelve months from its date; the said notes being overdue, this mortgage is given as additional security to another mortgage, dated the second day of October, 1851, and when the said notes and interest are paid then both mortgages are to be void.

Signed LEWIS JOSSELYN.

In witness. &c.

In presence of J. R. NEWHALL.

Recorded June 21st, 1852, fifteen minutes past 2 P. M.

I am credibly informed that a letter was received by Mr. Alley from Mr. Cushing, in substance, requesting him to come to Washington. Mr. Alley went to Washington, and Mr. Josselyn was appointed immediately after. The mortgage must be paid, but in the meantime, as appears above, was strengthened by another mortgage to the same gentleman, under date of June 14th, 1853, probably as a consideration for the office received.

I have the best information that the *Newburyport Union* newspaper was, at the time of the appointment of Mr. Colby, its editor, mortgaged to Hon. Caleb Cushing for the sum of seven hundred and fifty dollars, as follows:

Know all men by these presents, that we, Edwin Lawrence, William H. Huse and Joseph H. Bragdon, all of Newburyport, in the county of Essex, and Commonwealth of Massachusetts, for and in consideration of the sum of two hundred and fifty dollars, paid by CALEB CUSHING, of said Newburyport, the receipt whereof we hereby acknowledge, have granted, sold and assigned, and do by these presents grant, sell and assign unto the said CALEB CUSHING, the following described Goods and Chattels, viz., the materials of the Daily Union Printing Office, situated in the building numbered 36 in said State Street, with two Tufts Patent Printing Presses, nearly new, now in use in said office, (it being understood between the parties that said property is free of incumbrance saving and excepting a mortgage of eight hundred dollars to Charles Nason; on the third part of said goods and chattels belonging to said Edwin Lawrence, which said mortgage is not a lien upon the other two-thirds of said property.)

To have and to hold the aforedescribed Goods and Chattels to the said CALEB CUSHING, his executors, administrators and assigns forever. And we, the said Lawrence, Huse and Bragdon, do avouch ourselves to be the lawful owners of said goods and chattels, and have good right to sell and dispose of the same in manner aforesaid, excepting as above stated.

Provided, nevertheless, that if the said Edwin Lawrence, William H. Huse and Joseph H. Bragdon, their executors or administrators, shall pay unto the said CALEB CUSHING, his executors, administrators or assigns, the said sum of two hundred and fifty dollars, according to the tenor of a certain note of even date herewith, then this mortgage shall be void.

In witness whereof, we the said Lawrence, Huse and Bragdon, have subscribed the same this twenty-third day of January, in the year our Lord eighteen hundred and fifty.

Signed, EDWIN LAWRENCE,
WILLIAM H. HUSE,
JOSEPH H. BRAGDON.

Executed and delivered in presence of
ALBERT FRYE, GARDNER N. COBB.

Newburyport, Oct. 14, 1850, at 4 o'clock 25 minutes, P. M., received and recorded in the Book of Records of Mortgages, lib. 5 folio 174, and examined by Eleazer Johnson, Town Clerk.

A true copy of record.

Attest, ELEAZER JOHNSON, City Clerk.

Know all men by these presents, that we, Edwin Lawrence, William H. Huse and Joseph H. Bragdon, all of Newburyport, in the county of Essex, and Commonwealth of Massachusetts, for and in consideration of the sum of five hundred dollars paid by CALEB CUSHING, of said Newburyport, the receipt whereof we do hereby acknowledge, have granted, sold and assigned, and do by these presents grant, sell and assign unto the said CALEB CUSHING, the following described goods and chattels, viz., the type, presses and fixtures in the Newburyport Daily Union Office, at No. 3 State street, in said town, viz , one Adams Power Press, value $1000 ; two Tufts Patent Presses, value each $275 ; all type and fixtures used in the newspaper and job printing departments of said office, together with the books and accounts belonging to or pertaining to said office.

To have and to hold the aforedescribed goods and chattels to the said CALEB CUSHING, his executors, administrators and assigns forever. And we, the said Lawrence, Huse and Bragdon, do avouch ourselves to be the lawful owners of said goods and chattels, and have good right to sell and dispose of the same in manner aforesaid.

Provided, nevertheless, that if the said Lawrence, Huse and Bragdon, their executors or administrators, shall pay unto the said CALEB CUSHING, his executors, administrators or assigns, the said sum of five hundred dollars, according to the tenor of a certain note of hand of even date herewith, then this mortgage shall be void.

In witness whereof, we, the said Edwin Lawrence, William H. Huse and Joseph H. Bragdon, have subscribed the same, this eighth day of October, in the year of our Lord one thousand eight hundred and fifty.

Signed, EDWIN LAWRENCE,
WILLIAM H. HUSE,
JOSEPH H. BRAGDON.

Executed and delivered in presence of
F. LAWRENCE, J. Q. A. STONE.

Newburyport, Oct. 14, 1850, at 4 o clock 25 minutes, P. M., received and recorded in the Book of Records of Mortgages, lib. 5; folio 175, and examined by Eleazer Johnson, Town Clerk.

A true copy of record.

Attest, ELEAZER JOHNSON, City Clerk.

Another fact has come to my knowledge, proving Mr. Cushing's influence in the dispensing of patronage. The columns of the *Boston Times* exhibit long lists of lucrative government advertising. I have been informed upon undoubted evidence, that Caleb Cushing's name has been found as endorser upon the notes of George Roberts, the proprieter of that paper, and that Mr. Cushing has been forced to settle demands, brought against him in consequence. The advertising will now pay the notes. The *Times*, *Bay State* and *Union*, are all Coalition newspapers, and have thus been aided and sustained by Caleb Cushing. These appointments are Abolition appointments. Is the President responsible, or has Cushing deceived him? Is there any need of more proof of Cushing's Coalitionism? More can be found.

It is known that Mr Cushing made a show of opposing Chas. Sumner's election as Senator. It is not generally known that it was but a show. The Democratic State Convention met at Worcester on the 20th day of August, 1851. This was the first Convention of the party since the election of Chas. Sumner. Now was the proper time to pass a resolution of censure against that election. The National Democrats wished to do so. The coalitionists of course opposed. Gen. Cushing joined the last party, and *made a speech advocating harmony at any sacrifice.* This is the exact policy of the present administration, and shows who has deceived the President.—The National Democrats were beaten by Cushing and his Free Soil allies, and no resolution was passed. *Within a year General Cushing was appointed Judge of the Supreme Court by Gov. Boutwell, a coalitionist, and confirmed by a Free Soil Council.* Thus we behold General Cushing formally adopted into the coalition party, *receiving office from them; sustaining their policy in conventions; lending money on mortgage to their presses; assisting other Free Soil presses to pay mortgages to leading Free Soilers; and endorsing notes and giving patronage to proprietors of leading Coalition organs.* CAN A MAN BE MORE OF A COALITIONIST?

And now let us look at his course at Baltimore. Well known to be a friend of Hon. Robert Rantoul, Jr's, when the vote took place upon the right of Mr. Rantoul to a seat in the Convention, Mr. Cushing was *taken suddenly ill*, and remained so for two hours, until the question was decided, when he *as suddenly recovered.* Thus he left his seat to his substitute, a violent coalitionist, B. F. Butler of Lowell, who voted for Mr. Rantoul. Mr. Cushing was also forced to leave Baltimore for home before either nominee or platform was adopted, and even before Franklin Pierce had received *a single vote* for nomination, and thus the Convention lost his valuable services. This is his position at the present time. Let us glance at his opinions, as expressed in the past.

On the 27th and 28th of February, 1834, a series of resolutions were before the Massachusetts Legislature, on the subject of the administration of Andrew Jackson, and his removal of the deposits. Mr. Cushing made himself conspicuous by several speeches on the occasion, and thus poured out his bitterness on the President:

Doubtless the gentleman, or any other friend of the administration, who sees the President growing heady with unmerited elevation, intoxicated with flattery and power, and breaking forth into transports of ungovernable passion, would gladly shut his eyes to the humiliating proofs of his unfitness for the exalted station he occupies. [February 28. Mass. Legislature.]

And what is the style of this President of the people, this reforming and constitutional President? *That neither persuasion, nor coercion, nor the opinions of the people, nor the voice of the Legislature, could shake his fixed determination* Assuredly, arrogance like this, from the lips of a constitutional ruler, is alike unheard of and intolerable. Pray, what is the President? Is he some Asiatic despot lording it over his crouching slaves? Does he wield an hereditary sceptre? What giddy madness has seized upon a simple elected chief magistrate with limited constitutional functions, that he should dare thus to address the sovereign people in words of menace or dictation, and in the tone of a master? I, Andrew Jackson, have said it; my will shall be law; I care not for the miseries or the remonstrances of the people; I care not for Congress; I care not for the constitution. And this, forsooth, is the people's President, the democratic President? Phæton like he rashly throws himself into the chariot of State, and dashes blindly on, scattering dismay and ruin around him; but his disastrous career must and will end, although it is dealing forth terrible retribution on those who willed or suffered that he should govern the Union. [Feb. 28. Mass. Legislature.]

I have several extracts from his speeches on various occasions, which I propose to read, and shall proceed to take them up in connection with the Baltimore platform.—That being the creed of the Democratic party, and adopted by the President, upon his accepting the nomination, as the basis of his administration, let us glance at the peculiar fitness of Caleb Cushing to be his agent in carrying it out. The seventh resolution of the Baltimore Platform is as follows:

"That we are decidedly opposed to taking from the President the qualified veto power, by which he is enabled, under restrictions and responsibilities amply sufficient to guard the public interest, to suspend the passage of a bill whose merits cannot secure the approval of two-thirds of the Senate and House of Representatives until the judgment of the people can be obtained thereon, which has saved the American people from the corrupt and tyrannical domination of the Bank of the United States, and from a corrupting system of general internal improvements."

On February 27, 1834, Gen. Cushing, in the Massachusetts Legislature, thus holds forth:

"In the President's unparalleled exercise of the veto power, for but twice using which Louis XVI. was hurled by the French from his constitutional throne,—in his unparalleled disregard of the opinions of the Senate and House of Representatives, in the unparalleled political experiment he is now trying, at the expense of the people and the laws of the Union,—in all this the gentleman perceives the democratic character of the President. [See 7th Res. Balt. Platform.

The 6th section of the 3d resolution is as follows.

"That Congress has no power to charter a National Bank; that we believe such an institution one of deadly hostility to the best interests of the country, dangerous to our republican institutions and the liberties of the people, and calculated to place the business of the country within the control of a concentrated money power, and above the laws and the will of the people; and that the results of Democratic legislation in this and all other financial measures upon which issues have been made between the two political parties of the country, have demonstrated to candid and practical men, of all parties, their soundness, safety, and utility in all business pursuits."

The 7th section of the 3d resolution is as follows:

"That the separation of the monies of the Government from banking institutions is indispensable for the safety of the funds of the Government and the rights of the people."

Mr. Cushing, on the other hand, in his speech on the Post office Bill, delivered in the House of Representatives, August 25, 1841, thus holds forth:

"In that revolution Mr Cushing contended as he felt sure the gentleman from Tennessee, (Mr. Arnold) and the gentleman from Virginia (Mr. Botts,) contended for the success of great principles, and for the success of the men representing those principles, and in whose persons those principles should be embodied and made incarnate.—He contended for both. The individuals for whom he, in common with those gentlemen, had spoken, and written and labored, were placed in power, and therefore there is no question here as to men, but only as to principles; and if the allegation of the gentleman from Virginia is justified by the fact, it must be upon some question of principle that these men were to be charged with treachery to their party, to their friends and their country."—Speech on the Post Office bill, Aug. 25, 1841.

Mr C. admitted that throughout the controversy, at any rate wherever he was, and he addressed public assemblies in many of the States, and on numerous occasions, he admitted the Whig party condemned the currency measures of Mr. Van Buren's administration; they undertook to change its measures and to introduce better ones; they denounced the Sub Treasury.

Mr. C. said he had voted for both the Bank bills which had passed this House. He had done so, not because he approved entirely either of those bills, but because there was nothing in his past or present opinions to prevent him from acquiescing in that respect in the wishes of a majority of his political friends in the House. He believed, for himself, that a U. States Bank, duly constituted and with proper guards, was one, but not the only mode of settling the currency question."—Same Speech, page 8.

Finally we have swept from the statute book, not only the Sub Treasury act—the *sole* measure of Mr. Van Buren's administration—but also the Deposit act, the chief measure of General Jackson's second period; and have thus effectually put the stamp of the public reprobation upon all the financial policy of the last administrations.

May 20 and 21, 1840, Mr. Cushing delivered a speech in the House of Representatives against the sub-treasury and in favor of a National Bank.

Monday, Aug. 9, 1841—The bill to repeal the Sub-Treasury Law passed by 134 ayes to 87 noes—Mr. Cushing in the affirmative.

Monday, Aug. 23, 1841—The Fiscal Bank bill passed, 125 to 94—Mr. Cushing in the affirmative.

Friday, Sept. 10th—The vote on the passage of the Fiscal Bank bill, notwithstanding the President's veto, was 103 yeas to 71 nays—Mr. Cushing in the affirmative.

In the 6th resolution of the Baltimore Platform, the following opinions are expressed as the Democratic creed:

Resolved, That the proceeds of the Public Lands ought to be sacredly applied to the National objects specified in the Constitution; and that we are opposed to any law for the distribution of such proceeds among the States, as alike inexpedient in policy and repugnant to the Constitution.

Yet we find Mr. Cushing, in the speech before alluded to, thus declaiming:

"In the second place, we have passed the Land Distribution Bill, which in his, Mr. C.'s eye, if it had no other merit, was entitled to the highest consideration in being, at the same time, a permanent prospective pre-emption bill."

On Monday, May 23, 1836, the question pending, was the motion of Mr. Williams, of Kentucky, to refer the resolutions (of State of Kentucky on that subject) to the Committee of Ways and Means, with instructions to report a bill distributing the proceeds of the sales of the public lands among the several States, &c. Upon this Mr. Cushing addressed the House at great length, commencing: "He was favorable to a distribution of the revenue among the several States. He showed that there would be a surplus of some millions to divide." And upon a test motion to lay the instructions of Mr. Williams, with the resolutions, on the table, Mr Cushing voted *no*.

Jan. 14, 1836, Mr. Cushing introduced the following resolutions:

Resolved, That for the purpose of relieving the whole people of the United States from the inconveniences attending the present relation of the Federal Government to the Federal domain, and at the same time securing to the old and new States alike their just and lawful rights therein, the Select Committee on the Public Lands be instructed to consider the expediency of providing *for the division of the said domain among the several States* of the Union, according to the following principles, viz:

[Then follow seven sections, defining the manner.]

Tuesday, July 6, 1841, the Land Distribution Bill passed, 116 to 108, Mr. Cushing in the affirmative.

Again, on the same occasion, we find his opinions thus expressed on the Revenue Bill of 1841:

"Then we had passed the Revenue Bill, and he would say in regard to that, though he voted for it with extreme reluctance, on account of various objections of detail, and with the greater reluctance, because in that vote he differed from some of his respected colleagues, yet he thought it was due to principle that, at all hazards of personal or party popularity, we should not shamble on from indebtedness to indebtedness, and should at once provide means to meet the debts and carry on the business of the Government."

Yet the 4th section of the 3d resolution thus lays down the Democra'ic doctrine:

"That justice and sound policy forbid the Federal Government to foster one branch of industry to the detriment of any other, or to cherish the interests of one portion to the injury of any other portion of our common country."

Saturday, July 16, 1842. The vote on the Tariff Bill was 116 to 112, Mr. Cushing in the affirmative.

Wednesday, Aug, 17, 1842. The question being on the passage of the above bill, notwithstanding the President's veto, the vote was 91 to 87, Mr. Cushing in the affirmative.

On Monday, Aug. 22d, 1842, the Tariff Bill (the *High Tariff* of that year) passed by a vote of 105 to 103. Mr. Cushing in the affirmative.

I have thus shown the last known opinions of Caleb Cushing upon several of the subjects embraced in the Baltimore Platform. I have proved that so far as is known at the present time, he is a Whig upon those subjects; but one more remains. I accused him of being an Abolition agitator. I must give my reasons. We have found him the last few years a Coalitionist; let us see what he was from 1835 to the end of his Congressional career. It is well known that the agitation of the slavery question, then in its infancy, was carried on at that time under cover of the right of petition. Disunion petitions were presented in Congress, and the subject was agitated by the friends of abolition under the pretence of vindicating the right of petition. Let us follow Mr. Cushing in his course on this subject. Every vote on this subject I have collected, and will lay before you in a short summary, together with an extract from a speech of that gentleman on the 25th of January, 1836, and if you can find a stronger threat of agitation than is contained in that speech, then I am much mistaken.

Dec. 16, 1835, Mr. Fairfield, of Maine, presented an abolition petition. Laid on the table, 180 to 31; Pierce yes, Adams and *Cushing* in the negative.

Motion to print laid on the table; 168 to 50; Pierce yes, Adams and *Cushing* no.

Friday, Dec. 18, 1835, Mr. Jackson, of Mass., presented an abolition petition. Dec. 21, 1835, this came up and was laid on the table, 140 to 76. Pierce voting yes, Adams, *Cushing*, Jackson and Hoar voting no.

Dec. 23, 1835, a similar petition was laid on the table, 144 to 67. Pierce yes, Adams and *Cushing* no.

Jan. 6, 1836, Mr. Jarvis, of Maine, moved (in substance) that "this House ought not to entertain abolition petitions." It was moved to lay this on the table. Not carried, 66 to 123. Adams and *Cushing* voted yes.

Jan. 13, 1836, a motion to lay the above on the table failed again. 58 to 156. Adams, *Cushing* and Hoar, voting yes, F. Pierce no.

Jan. 25. Motion to lay the question of receiving an abolition petition on the table, passed 143 to 44. F. Pierce yes, Adams, *Cushing*, &c., no.

Speech of C. Cushing on the Right of Petition for the Abolition of Slavery and the Slave Trade in the District of Columbia, January 25, 1836.

We have been told that the prayer of the petitioners is for a thing which the Constitution does not permit to Congress, and so the petition itself should not be received. I ask the House how it appears that we have no right, by the Constitution, to legislate upon the subject matter of the petition? It may be so, and it may not. One member of the House has earnestly averred that it is, another that it is not. Which of them is right? I confess, for myself, that I cannot think it becomes the House to decide either way, upon the mere *ipse dixit* of individual members. Besides, the petition calls in question not only slavery, but also the *commerce in slaves*. And will any gentleman affirm that the slave trade of the District is among those holy things which Congress may not constitutionally handle? Is this District set apart by the Constitution, under whatever changes of opinion or fact the progress of civilization may introduce, to be unchangeably and forever a general slave market for the rest of the Union? I confess, that I, again, am disappointed in that. Among all the confident things said in denial of the constitutional powers of Congress in this matter, there has not been, so far as I remember, any systematic argument on the perfectly distinct branches of the double constitutional question involved in it, namely—the slave property and the slave traffic in this District *And what shall be said of our constitutional power in the purchased territories under the jurisdiction of the United States,* [Is not this the Wilmot Proviso?] to which some of these petitions apply? And what clause of the Constitution restricts the right of petition to constitutional things? This house cannot grant beyond its powers; these are limited by the Constitution; but the people may petition for anything; for the right of petition is, by the Constitution, secured for ever against any and every limitation or restriction.

* * * * * *

Men of Virginia, countrymen of Washington, of Patrick Henry, of Jefferson, of Madison, will ye be true to your constitutional faith? Men of New York, will ye ride over the principles of the Democracy ye profess? Men of the West, can ye prove recreant to the spirit of sturdy independence which carried you beyond the mountains? Men of New England, I hold you to the doctrines of liberty which ye inherit from your Puritan forefathers. And if *this House is to be scared by whatever influence, from its duty to receive and hear the petitions of the people,* THEN I SHALL SEND MY VOICE BEYOND THE WALLS OF THIS CAPITOL FOR REDRESS. To the people I say, your liberties are in danger; they whom you have chosen to be your representatives are untrue to their trust! *Come ye to the rescue!* for the vindication of your right of petition, to you I appeal; to you, the people who sent us here, whose agents we are, and to whom we shall return to render a reckoning of our stewardship, and who are the true and only sovereigns in this republic.

On Feb. 8th, 1836, the question arising to refer all petitions, &c., to a select Committee, Mr. Cushing voted yes.

Immediately after, the second part of the resolution coming up as follows—" with instructions to report that Congress possesses no constitutional authority to interfere in any way with the institution of slavery in any of the States of this confederacy "—Mr. Cushing had *stepped out*, and his name is not found recorded.

On the third branch—" And that in the opinion of this House, Congress ought not to interfere in any way with slavery in the district of Columbia "—Mr. Cushing reappears with Adams, Jackson and Phillips, voting no to the above.

And on the fourth branch—" Because it would be a violation of the public faith, unwise, impolitic and dangerous to the Union " —Mr. Cushing voted against its adoption, with his brother Abolitionists, Adams, Jackson and Phillips—while upon the whole of the above F. Pierce is found in the affirmative.

May 26, 1836, on the following:—*Resolved,* That Congress ought not to interfere in any way with slavery in the District of Columbia—Franklin Pierce voted yes, Cushing, Jackson, Phillips, &c., no; and upon the resolve to lay all petitions, &c., on the table without further action, Franklin Pierce voted yes, Cushing and friends no.

Monday, Dec. 26, 1836, Mr. Adams presented a petition for the abolition of slavery and the slave trade in the District of Columbia, which was laid on the table, 116 to 36. Franklin Pierce in the affirmative; Adams, Cushing, Jackson in the negative.

January 9, 1837, Mr. Adams presented another similar petition, which was tabled, 150 to 50. Pierce voted yes; Cushing, Adams and Phillips no.

Jan. 18, 1837, Mr. Hawes moved that "all Abolition petitions, &c., be laid on the table without being printed or referred, and that no further action be had thereon," upon which Franklin Pierce voted yes; Cushing, Adams, Phillips, voted no. 129 to 69. Passed.

On Saturday, Feb. 11, 1837, the House voted 160 to 35 against receiving a petition from slaves, as it would be " disregarding its own dignity, the rights of a large class of citizens of the South and West, and the Constitution of the United States." Upon this last quoted Franklin Pierce voted aye, Cushing, Adams, Jackson and Phillips voted no.

Tuesday, Dec. 12, 1837, Mr. Adams presented a petition for the abolition of slavery in the District of Columbia. Laid on the table, 135 to 70. Adams, *Cushing*, Phillips voted *no*.

Thursday, Dec. 21, 1837, Mr. Patton having moved in substance that all abolition petitions should be laid on the table without further notice, *Cushing* and Phillips voted *no*.

On the 11th day of December, 1838, Charles G. Atherton, of New Hampshire, introduced a series of resolutions into the House of Representatives, to the reception of which Caleb Cushing objected, but which were admitted under a suspension of the rules in spite of his objection, and among which were the following:

2. *Resolved*, That petitions for the abolition of slavery in the District of Columbia and in the Territories of the United States, and against the removal of slaves from one State to another, are a part of a plan of operations set on foot to affect the institution of slavery in the several States, and thus indirectly to destroy that institution within their limits.

3. *Resolved*, That Congress has no right to do that indirectly which it cannot do directly; and that the agitation of the subject of slavery in the District of Columbia, or the Territories, as a means, and with the view, of disturbing or overthrowing that institution in the several States, is against the true spirit and meaning of the Constitution, an infringement of the rights of the States affected, and a breach of the public faith upon which they entered into the confederacy.

5. *Resolved, therefore*, That all attempts on the part of Congress to abolish Slavery in the District of Columbia or the Territories, or to prohibit the removal of slaves from State to State, or to discriminate between the institutions of one portion of the confederacy and another, with the views aforesaid, are in violation of the Constitution, destructive of the fundamental principle on which the Union of these States rests, and beyond the jurisdiction of Congress; and that every petition, memorial, resolution, proposition or paper, touching or relating in any way, or to any extent whatever, to slavery as aforesaid, or the abolition thereof, shall, on the presentation thereof, without any further action thereon, be laid upon the table, without being debated, printed or referred.

These resolutions introduced by Mr. Atherton, of New Hampshire, in whose recent election as Senator, Gen. Pierce interested himself so actively, were received by a suspension of the rules in the face of an objection by Caleb Cushing, and upon each and every one of these, his vote (Mr. C's.) is found recorded in the negative, with Adams, Giddings and other abolitionists.

On Friday, Dec. 21, 1838, Mr. Cushing moved to amend the journal as follows:

Insert therein—"Mr. Cushing presented a petition from Joseph Young and others, of Salisbury, in the State of Massachusetts, which was laid on the table under Mr. Atherton's resolutions; and on presenting the same Mr. Cushing protested that in submitting to the application of said rule to this petition, he yielded not to power, conceiving said resolution not to be constitutional, and, therefore, in itself purely null and void; but which motion the Speaker decided to be out of order."

Which motion was rejected, 14 to 174, Adams, Cushing, Giddings, in the affirmative.

On Dec. 13, 1838, Mr. Slade, of Vermont, submitted the following:

Whereas, There exists and is carried on between the ports in the District of Columbia, and other parts of the United States, and under the sanction of the laws thereof, a trade in human beings, whereby thousands of them are annually sold and transported from said District to distant parts of the country, in vessels belonging to citizens of the United States, and whereas such trade involves an outrageous violation of human rights, is a disgrace to the country by whose laws it is sanctioned, and calls for immediate interposition of legislative authority for its suppression; therefore to the end that all obstacles to the consideration of this subject may be removed, and a remedy for the evil speedily provided,

Resolved, That so much of the fifth resolution of the subject of slavery, passed by this House on the 11th and 12th of the present month, as relates to the 'removal of slaves from State to State,' and prohibits the action of this House on 'every petition, memorial, resolution, proposition or paper touching' the same, be and hereby is rescinded.

Objections being made, Mr. S. moved a suspension of the rules, and Adams and *Cushing* and Giddings voted for a suspension unsuccessfully.

Mr. Calhoun of Kentucky, introduced a resolution, the same day, to make it unlawful to aid fugitive slaves to escape, and on a suspension of the rules to receive this, Messrs. Adams and *Cushing* voted *no*, while, strange to say, Giddings could not go so far, but voted *yes*.

On Monday, January 7th, 1839, Mr. Cushing presented the petition of Peter Sanborn and others, of Reading, in the State of Massachusetts, praying the House to rescind the resolution of the 12th of December last, and moved that said memorial, together with the resolves of the State of Massachusetts on the right of petition and debate, presented to the House on the 28th of May last, and not finally acted on by the House, be referred to the committee of the whole on the state of the Union, with instructions to consider the expediency of adopting the following resolutions, viz. Then follow four resolutions, the three first of which state in substance that the right of petition and debate is a right guaranteed by the Constitution, and that Congress has no right to limit it, and the fourth and last resolution is as follows:

Resolved, therefore, That all that part of a certain resolution of the House of Representatives adopted on the 12th day of December last, which provides that "every petition, memorial, resolution, proposition or paper," of a prescribed class, "shall, on the presentation thereof, without any further action thereon, be laid on the table without being debated, printed or referred," is a violation of the rights of the States, whose official communications of said class it excludes from due and proper consideration; a violation of the right of petition inherent in the people of the United States, which it cancels and abridges, and a violation of the privilege of speech and of debate, rightfully appertaining to the members of this House, which it forecloses and abolishes; and therefore that so much of the resolution be and the same is hereby declared unconstitutional and merely void, and of null effect. [Mr. Cushing wished to debate]

Dec. 30, 1839, Mr. Wise's Resolution (Atherton's) being before the House, Mr. Cushing voted against suspending the Rules to receive it.

Dec 31, on Mr. Coles's (the same purport) Mr. Cushing voted no, as also on Mr. Wise's a second time.

Jan 14, 1840, Mr. Thompson of S. C. offering the same, Mr. Cushing voted in the negative.

Jan. 28, 1840, Mr. Adams offered a resolution which was amended on motion of Mr. Johnson of Maryland, by striking out all after the word resolved, and inserting a resolve against entertaining abolition petitions "in any way whatever." On this latter resolve Adams, *Cushing* and Giddings voted *no*.

Dec. 23, 1840, Mr. James of Pennsylvania presented an abolition petition, and moved a suspension of the Rules that it might be received. Mr. W. Cost Johnson moved to lay this on the table. Upon this Adams, *Cushing* and Giddings voted *no*.

June 7, 1841, Mr. Adams offered an amendment to a resolution of Mr. Wise, which was to strike out the 21st rule, [Mr. Atherton's in substance] upon which the vote was 112 yes, to 104 no. Messrs. Adams, *Cushing*, Giddings, in the affirmative. June 10, 1841, upon a motion to reconsider the above, Messrs. Adams, *Cushing* and Giddings voted no.

On June 14, 1841, on a motion to reconsider, the vote was 106 ayes to 104 nays, Adams, Cushing and Giddings, in the negative. June 15, 1841, the question recurring, Mr. Cushing made a speech against the previous question, and in favor of Mr. Adams, and on the vote upon Mr. Adams's amendment of June 7 again being taken, it was rejected, 106 to 110. Adams, *Cushing* and Giddings in the affirmative.

Dec. 14, 1841, Mr. Adams presented an abolition petition, which he moved to refer to a select committee. On motion to lay this on the table, Adams, *Cushing* and Giddings voted no.

On Tuesday, Jan. 4, 1842, Mr. Adams's motion of Dec. 14, 1841, coming up, was laid on the table, 115 to 84. Adams, *Cushing* and Giddings in the negative. Some twenty other petitions arising were laid on the table by different votes, Adams, *Cushing* and Giddings always in the negative.

Jan. 18, 1842, Mr. Henry presented an abolition petition, which was laid on the table, 93 to 75, Adams, *Cushing* and Giddings in the negative.

Dec. 6, 1842, Mr. Adams moved to rescind the 21st rule. Upon laying this on the table, Messrs. Adams, *Cushing* and Giddings voted no.

Dec. 8, 1842, Mr. Adams's motion of Dec. 6 coming up, on motion to lay it on the table, Adams, *Cushing* and Giddings, voted no.

Dec. 12, 1842, the motion to lay Mr. Adams's motion of Dec 6, 1842, on the table again recurring, it was carried, 106 to 102, Adams, *Cushing* and Giddings, again in the negative.

It will be found on referring to the Baltimore Platform, that this is directly opposed to the fourth and fifth resolutions of that Convention.

But it may be said, Mr. Cushing has changed his opinions since then. How do we know? The latest recorded opinions, which I have been able to obtain, of Mr. Cushing's, are such as have been quoted just now, and where is the proof that he has changed? Mr. Cushing remained comparatively quiet after the administration of Mr. Tyler, till, in 1847, owing to his warm adoption of the policy of the Mexican war, the Democratic Convention of Massachusetts nominated him for Governor. It occasioned a great deal of dissatisfaction at the time. How well the party liked it, and how well they supported him, may be found in the fact, that out of 54,228 votes, which the Democrats of Massachusetts threw in 1844 for George Bancroft for Governor, Mr. Cushing received at his first trial—in 1847—but 39,398, and, upon further reflection, but 26,695 voters were induced to support him, and his further nomination became impossible, save at the certain risk of the utter disorganization of the party. The Democrats of Massachusetts *know* Caleb Cushing too well to place any confidence in him. It was with this brand upon him that he entered General Pierce's Cabinet.

And now he is attempting to regulate the future course of the Democratic party. Let us see what his idea of a political party is. In 1841 he was in the full tide of success. The Whigs had achieved a victory, and he was the official spokesman. As such, in his speech of August 25, 1841, he defines his ideas of a party:

"It was upon the broad and great platform of opposition to the administration, and of conciliation toward each other, that the members of the Whig party, *entertaining themselves opinions of every shade of difference*, and associated in their past history with every diversity of party, — it was upon this lofty platform that they had planted the banner of Harrison and Tyler, and rallied around it as the great symbol of union and of victory for the whole people of the United States."

Again after stating that he voted for both Bank bills, he says:

"But whilst himself pursuing this course, he did not conceive that, because any gentleman might have happened to differ from him, therefore he had any right to denounce any such gentleman. He abjured, for instance, all claim of right to denounce the gentleman from Kentucky, (Mr. Marshall,) or his colleague from Massachusetts, (Mr. Adams,) because they had seen fit to vote against the first Bank bill. They had put their votes upon considerations of conscience and honor; he believed them to be sincere then, and he believed so still. Thus putting their votes upon their conscience and honor, though thus differing from the great body of their friends, no man had a right to arraign their conduct, or insinuate any charge of treachery. And in the same way that those two gentlemen had a right to differ with their party associates on the Bank bill, so had his colleagues, (Mr. Winthrop and Mr. Saltonstall,) in regard to the Revenue bill. So also had the gentlemen from Georgia a right to act on their separate judgment of the Land bill; and the gentlemen from Kentucky and Virginia on the Bankrupt bill. So he contended was the President of the United States entitled to the same right of conscience, and to exercise the same privilege of individual judgment in his legislative action, on bills presented to him by Congress, and to approve them or not, according to his conscientious convictions of what is or is not constitutional or just."

This is his idea of what a party should be—"composed of every shade of difference of opinion,"

"Black spirits and white, blue spirits and gray,
Mingle, mingle, mingle—ye that mingle may."

This is what he wishes the Democratic party to be. This is what he has deceived the President into adopting, and for this purpose, feeling that the Democratic party will resent this policy, he is about to hurry the administration into a war—as is evident from his remarks at Newark—that in the glory of successful military achievements the errors of the Cabinet may be forgotten. This, gentlemen, is the *Mexican discipline* Brigadier General Cushing wishes to enforce upon the Democratic party. The head of the party is to be thrust into Free Soil for his benefit. The party is to be broken up, that renegade Whigs may stand upon a level with tried Democrats.

But it will be said we are opposing the President. But no, we are opposing the Cabinet, and those who have stolen in there by deception. And if we were opposing the administration, let me refer Mr. Cushing to his own ideas of Democracy, as portrayed in his speech of February 27th, 1834, in the Massachusetts Legislature:

"Sir, one gentleman who opposed the consideration of them, has reproached us with 'oppugnation to the powers that be,' and he tauntingly demanded of us 'whether it be pleasant for old Massachusetts always to be in a minority?' And whether she is content to 'lose influence' by expressing opinions unpalatable to the administration? When, afterwards, I heard the same gentleman talk of principles, of his principles, of democratic principles, I could not but consider, with something of wonder, though with more of amusement, the inconsistency of his professions upon this head. Are we to laud the President to the skies, right or wrong, in order to obtain credit at Washington? Is this principle? Are we to chain our consciences and our opinions to the car of a triumphant military chieftain? Are we to kiss the mailed heel that treads upon our necks, and tramples us into the earth? Is this 'democracy?' So have not I learned democracy. I had strangely imagined that we were to act conscientiously, according to our conscientious convictions; that we should not palter with duty by stifling its voice; and that, minority though we might be, in reference to the present administration, we enjoyed the consolatory consciousness of obeying the dictates of a high and solemn regard for the constitutional liberties of the land. If to sacrifice principles, conscience, duty, for the sake of 'influence' with the executive, be the 'democracy' of which that gentleman speaks, I desire none of it; and of the party success he flourishes before us, we may say, as the old Roman did, 'Victrix causa diis placuit, sed victa Catoni.'"

And now, gentlemen, I am done. I started by asserting that Caleb Cushing was a Whig, a Coalitionist, and an abolition agitator. I have laid my proofs before you, and you must judge. And now, what shall be done? Shall we yield to the pressure around us! Shall Mr. Cushing force us into Coalitionism?—Proscribed at Washington, read out of the party at home, shall we yield one jot or one tittle of the principle we have adopted? No! no!! a thousand times no!!! Let us keep up our organization. Let us nominate our candidates. Let us nail our flag to the mast, and wait for better times. Yet, Democrats,

"Your banner torn but flying,
Streams like the thunder storm *against* the wind;
Your trumpet voice, though broken now and dying,
The loudest still—the tempest leaves behind.
Your tree hath lost its blossoms, and the rind,
Chopped by the axe, looks rough and little worth;
But the sap lasts, and still the seed we find,
Sown deep, even in the bosom of the north;
So shall a better Spring less bitter fruit bring forth."

www.ingramcontent.com/pod-product-compliance
Lightning Source LLC
LaVergne TN
LVHW010833120826
845149LV00016B/1335

* 9 7 8 1 4 1 8 1 9 0 0 3 3 *